GW00373790

Haggai

MOTIVATING GOD'S PEOPLE

CWR

Steve Bishop

Contents

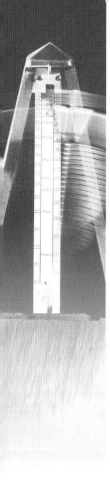

Introduction

'Motivation' is a key element in today's competitive world. Self-motivation is often seen as the ideal. But other influences can be quick to 'kick in' when this seems lacking. Parents strive to motivate their children to achieve good exam results. Employers urge their workforce to 'up' their output. Sports coaches shout at their teams to give '110%'. Charities plead with local communities for even more social engagement in its many expressions. These snapshots show a trend: people need help to get started and maintain momentum.

The lack of 'drive' is not a failing limited to twenty-first century, Western society. Nor is it only to be seen outside the community of 'committed' Christians – those who believe that a relationship with God is not simply attending a Sunday service. Israel, back in the Old Testament, presents a graphic illustration of God's people with problems in this area. That's probably an understatement. Throughout their history they displayed an ongoing inclination to do nothing – or worse – in terms of following God. Their default position was a stubbornness in wanting their own way, and failing to see the disastrous consequences of doing so.

Lacking drive

The account of Israel's formative years showed this self-interest to be top of their agenda. They did not have any ongoing motivation in seriously following God. Even when in the desert, having miraculously escaped from Egyptian slavery, they moaned about the conditions, longing to return to the land of the pharaohs. Their amazing survival through 40 years of wilderness wandering and being brought into the Promised Land failed to impress them. Within two generations of the passing of Moses and Joshua – their great leaders – they were following the abhorrent practices of the local religions. The 'drive' to be true to God was noticeably lacking.

Events reached a climax when the Israelites demanded a king to rule over them. They had looked around, not 'up'. Noticing that neighbouring countries all had a monarchy, they were motivated to have the same, particularly wanting an army commander. So Samuel, their judge-leader under God, was instructed to anoint Saul into that position. He was the first of a succession of kings. Their spiritual condition spanned a wide spectrum. Some followed God to varying degrees, others defiantly turned against Him.

Restoration

It was the continuing and underlying waywardness of God's people that resulted in the nation eventually fragmenting. Ten tribes split away from the other two, forming their own kingdom and system of worship. Although the remaining tribes (collectively named 'Judah') nominally followed God, their ongoing stubbornness led to disaster. They, like those ten tribes some years previously, were eventually swallowed up by the 'super power' of their day. However, unlike those other tribes, they remained an identifiable entity. They may have then been driven away from the Promised Land, but not from God's sight or reach.

After a period of exile, God started to fulfil the prophecies that He had previously given. His people, amazingly, were allowed by the regime in power to return to their homeland and, in particular, to Jerusalem. This restoration took place under the leadership of men called by God. They were noticeably motivated in readily responding to Him and the different roles given to them. Haggai was one of these men who were used by God to 'pick up the pieces'. The details of his brief but vital contribution in galvanising God's people are the subject of the Old Testament prophecy bearing his name.

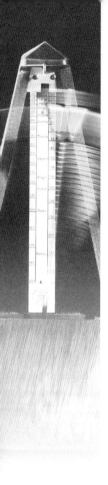

What is it?

But what makes up 'motivation'? How can the ingredients then be used to stimulate action? The basic principles have not changed. They are best encapsulated by the words 'carrot' and 'stick'. This was particularly evident in processes that I once evaluated in a government department. It involved social security benefits for the unemployed. There were various requirements in receiving such payments. These included undertaking training courses, attending review meetings with advisors, and searching for jobs. The 'carrot' element of this process was simple. All the courses, advice and computer facilities were free and professionally sourced. For well-motivated claimants these were very positive 'drivers'. However, some jobseekers lacked such motivation. So for them there was a 'stick' approach. Sanctions could be considered when required action was not taken, including benefit payments being affected.

God's ways of motivating us can, broadly speaking, fall into similar categories. He has a large variety of 'carrots' and 'sticks'. Haggai's prophecy describes some of these in action. However, their application is not restricted to the distant past or to the Jews in a faraway location. The message from God through Haggai is also relevant to us. Reading through this study will help us to have our hearts, minds and wills focused on following God and keeping it up without the need for corrective persuasion. Or at least we will recognise it if God needs to bring it into operation!

But there is an important factor to remember. Unlike a government department or other source of persuasion, God's interaction is always undergirded by His love and compassion. When His people were definitely not in a 'good place', God once spoke to them through His prophet. These words are also directed to us: 'I have loved you with an everlasting love; I have drawn you with unfailing kindness' (Jer. 31:3).

WEEK ONE

God's Diary

Icebreaker

Look at your diary – electronic or otherwise – and discuss the different reasons behind making those appointment entries. For instance, were they imposed and non-negotiable, or were they entirely within your power to arrange and prioritise?

Bible Readings

- Haggai 1:1–2
- Psalm 90
- Psalm 139
- Jeremiah 1:1–10
- Matthew 24:36–44
- Galatians 4:1–7

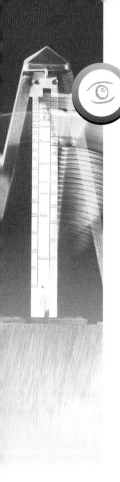

Opening Our Eyes

'I'll need to check if I'm free.' This is often said when trying to make an appointment. In whatever context it's spoken, it points to one thing – the diary. For some people this may constitute scribbled notes on a kitchen wall calendar. Others might use more sophisticated technology!

God also has a 'diary'. Or, at least, He has an agenda when events are to take place. This world's 'clock' started 'ticking' when the eternal God spoke the words, 'Let there be light' (Gen. 1:3). The salvation of humanity through Jesus' incarnation was a particularly significant date. It was one specifically laid down: 'But when the set time had fully come, God sent his Son' (Gal. 4:4). There is another major 'date' that's been set. This is when Jesus will return as Lord of lords. However, it's one that's unknown. Only our Father in heaven has access to that knowledge (Matt. 24:36).

God's people also featured in His 'diary'. Following years of obdurate apostasy and rebellion, the northern kingdom, which had split away from the dynasty of King David, was overwhelmed by its enemies. The Assyrian Empire swallowed and thoroughly digested its inhabitants in 722 BC. They were followed in 586 BC by the Jews who constituted the remaining nation of 'Judah'. But this time it was the Babylonian super power who took over. Despite being in forced exile, these Jews retained their separate identity.

Although it was a dark time in their history, a prophecy through Jeremiah regarding a return to their homeland was wonderfully fulfilled. This was through the decree of Cyrus, the Persian emperor (the Babylonians having been overthrown). It allowed them to return home. The date in God's 'diary' was 538 BC.

News of this release was evidently not greeted with great enthusiasm by the Jews. Certainly not by the majority. Motivation, or the lack of it, was the key factor. The prospect of a tricky journey back through hostile territory to Jerusalem, whose protective walls were now in ruins, was not a positive one. They were going to be in a very vulnerable environment. But under the leadership of Sheshbazzar, son of the exiled king of Judah, Jehoiachin (Ezra 1:11), a relatively small number of around fifty thousand did trek back (Ezra 2:64). Zerubbabel, also from the family line of David (featured in Jesus' lineage in Matt. 1:12), became the next governor sometime after their arrival home. Alongside him was Joshua (or Jeshua) the priest.

But having returned home, the Jews found it hard going. Although work commenced on constructing another Temple in Jerusalem in 536 BC, it barely got beyond the foundations being laid. Outside forces brought pressure to bear so that reconstruction was halted (Ezra 4:4–24). In the ensuing years, the factors giving rise to this inactivity were not only external. God's people got distracted and lacked motivation.

But the 'dates' in God's 'diary' then showed another significant entry. 'In the second year of King Darius, on the first day of the sixth month, the word of the LORD came through the prophet Haggai' (Hag. 1:1). God had not been unaware of events or what needed to be done. On a specific day (in 520 BC) He spoke to Haggai, His appointed prophet. As we will read in our next study, God was not happy! The words subsequently directed to the Jews proved to be a source of motivation, both 'carrot' and 'stick'. They came at a specified time; God's agenda was made clear.

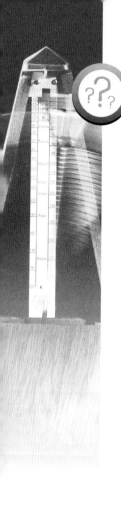

Discussion Starters

1. Haggai noticed and recorded when God spoke. Do you find it helpful to maintain a record of significant events or experiences in your spiritual journey, and the dates when they occur? Why or why not?

_____

_____

_____

_____

_____

2. God is eternal and is not restricted by time. Why, then, do you think He chooses to operate within a framework of time as we understand it?

_____

_____

_____

_____

_____

3. What factors may have determined when God spoke to Haggai? What does this reveal to us about God's character?

_____

_____

_____

_____

_____

4. What assurance did the psalmist find in God, saying: 'all the days ordained for me were written in your book' (Psa. 139:16)?

_____

_____

_____

_____

_____

5. The psalmist stated that God 'knit me together in my mother's womb' (Psa. 139:13). How does this assure you about God's timing and purposes for your life?

_____

_____

_____

_____

_____

6. Why did the psalmist warn us about careful use of time (Psa. 90:12–15)?

_____

_____

_____

_____

_____

7. In what ways can the brevity of life described in Psalm 90:1–6 be a powerful motivator?

_____

_____

_____

_____

_____

8. Do you feel that it's important for us to set aside regular time in prayer and Bible reading? Why or why not?

_____

_____

_____

_____

_____

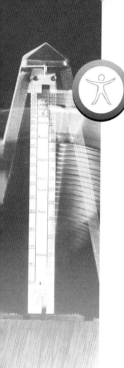

Personal Application

Time itself can be a motivation. However, it's not the dates in our diaries, or the passage of time on clocks that's important. It's the timing to which God is working that's vital. We are not very good at recognising that factor of God's control. Jeremiah wrote about this: 'Even the stork in the sky knows her appointed seasons, and the dove, the swift and the thrush observe the time of their migration. But my people do not know the requirements of the LORD' (Jer. 8:7).

Submitting to God's timing can be a challenge, but it's one that we are called to. Being aware of our own responsibility in using time, and reminding ourselves that God has perfect plans and is ultimately in control, can be key motivators for us in following Him and pursuing His purposes for our lives.

Seeing Jesus in the Scriptures

The Gospel accounts of Jesus' life and work include specific occasions when He interacted with people. He was aware that bringing God's touch to people had a time element. When shown to a man born blind, He stated: 'As long as it is day, we must do the works of him who sent me. Night is coming, when no one can work' (John 9:4). Jesus was working to God's agenda and timing.

WEEK TWO

Probing Questions

Icebreaker

Reflect on the different situations and conversations of the past week. What kind of questions, either your own or directed to you, were asked? What were the underlying reasons for them? For instance, was there a genuine interest in the answer or was it asked out of politeness or protocol?

Bible Readings

- Haggai 1:2–4
- Isaiah 40:12–31
- Genesis 3:8–13
- John 5:1–15
- Mark 9:33–37
- Mark 10:46–52

Opening Our Eyes

Questions form an integral part of our daily conversations. Whatever the scenario or subject under discussion, there will inevitably be questions that are raised. That's particularly evident where people are meeting for the first time, or after a lengthy period of absence. A barrage of questions is likely to be exchanged in order to obtain or update on vital information. But questions are not asked for the same reason or identical motives. Two friends would be finding out about each other in an entirely different manner to that of motorists whose cars have collided!

The interesting fact that emerges from the Bible is that God is also recorded as asking questions... a surprisingly large number. These are directed both at specific groups and at individuals. Clearly they are not being raised because He is ignorant of information or unaware of motives behind a course of action. He is the Lord Almighty, having complete knowledge and able to scrutinise every heart. So the reason for Him making enquiries is not for His own benefit. Rather, they are for the benefit of those to whom they are being directed. They are to address specific issues in the lives of people, and that's generally not good news in the first instance!

Unnerved

In addition, God does not mince His words. The question that He instructed Haggai to bring to His people was to be prefaced with a concise statement. It was actually an echo of what the Jews had said to themselves: 'These people say, "The time has not yet come to rebuild the LORD's house"' (Hag. 1:2). This, of itself, should have unnerved them. God had been overhearing their conversations or even reading their minds. Somewhat in the style of another Old Testament prophet named Malachi, God was picking up on what He'd heard and bringing a devastating retort by way of a question. He had clearly felt the 'pulse' of their hearts. His people lacked any motivation to rebuild the Temple and focus on Him.

So God's ensuing question was probably not a surprise: 'Is it a time for you yourselves to be living in your panelled houses, while this house remains a ruin?' (Hag. 1:4). Perhaps this was an over-statement since such elaborate furnishing would have been limited to royal properties. But it clearly indicated that God was able to inspect their interior designs and note the expense and effort that had been invested. His rhetorical question was thereby all the more probing and disconcerting.

Not giving up

The statement and question had initially been spoken to those in leadership. These were Zerubbabel the governor and Joshua the high priest. But they were representative of the people now living in Jerusalem and Judah. God was taking the first step to make everyone aware that He knew what was going on, and that things needed to change! It was amazing that God should bother to ask a question. This 'wake-up call' had therefore also clearly indicated that He had not given up on them. That itself was a means of motivation. The Jews were alerted through this question to stop what they were doing, step back and reassess their priorities – quickly!

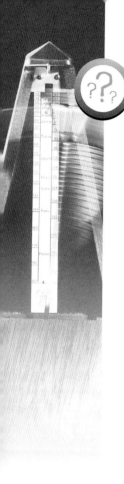

Discussion Starters

1. How does God's rhetorical question in Haggai 1:4 lead you to imagine how His people had been living?

2. Why do you think the Jews had failed to prioritise the rebuilding of the Lord's house?

3. Why can questions be a particularly good tool in challenging and motivating?

4. God spoke through Isaiah to the people of Israel, who were struggling to recognise His power. In what way were these rhetorical questions helping them refocus (Isa. 40:18–31)?

5. God also spoke through Isaiah to bring motivation in trusting Him. Why did God begin by apparently quoting back a question that the people were themselves asking (Isa. 40:27)?

_____

_____

_____

_____

6. What was God motivating Adam to do when asking him the first recorded question: 'Where are you?' (Gen. 3:9)? Why did God prompt Adam in this way?

_____

_____

_____

7. What do you consider were the reasons for Jesus asking the paralysed man, 'Do you want to get well?' (John 5:6)?

_____

_____

_____

_____

8. What motivation do you feel was brought to blind Bartimaeus when Jesus asked the question: 'What do you want me to do for you?' (Mark 10:51)?

_____

_____

_____

_____

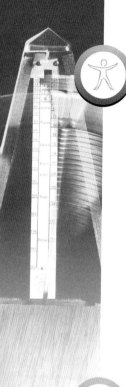

Personal Application

There is a tendency to think that God speaks only in certain ways. These include issuing instructions, providing guidance, bringing encouragement and giving reminders of His qualities.

But these verses in Haggai show that God also speaks by asking questions. We may well approach God with our own demanding questions, but equally He can come to us with His! As the Hebrews of Haggai's time realised, they are the means of challenging us regarding issues requiring attention. The questions that other people may ask us regarding our actions, decisions and motives may also have been prompted by God. They, together with the many other ways by which God speaks, could be the initial means of motivating us to take note of something as a prelude to change.

Seeing Jesus in the Scriptures

On one occasion Jesus declared: 'I do nothing on my own but speak just what the Father has taught me' (John 8:28). It is clear that questions were integral to Jesus' ministry, as were those of His Father. What Haggai was instructed to direct to God's people reflected what was to take place 500 years later and with equally probing intentions. Jesus once asked His disciples, 'What were you arguing about on the road?' (Mark 9:33). Their response was an uneasy silence. They had disputed which of them was to be the greatest. Motivation to have the right attitude and put God first again needed to be addressed, just as in Haggai's time.

WEEK THREE

Facing Facts

Icebreaker

Make a list of the different words and terms used in the world of education, sport and employment that denote equipping and preparing. What aspect of that activity does each one stress?

Bible Readings

- Haggai 1:5–11
- 1 Corinthians 5
- 2 Corinthians 2:5–11
- 2 Timothy 2:1–7
- Titus 2:11–15
- Hebrews 12:4–11

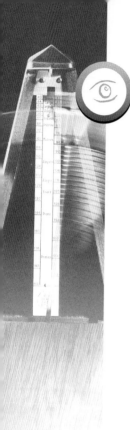

Opening Our Eyes

'Discipline' is not a fashionable word as far as society is concerned! It might be regarded by some as not politically correct. Yet it is still practised across a broad spectrum of life experiences. A football team coach may demand that players undertake extra training sessions because of a string of defeats. A teacher may require a student to submit additional work on account of poor exam results. An employer could direct a worker to undergo remedial supervision arising from inadequate performance. A motorist may be instructed to attend an offenders' driving scheme following road traffic offences.

These examples, it may be noted, are not intended as punishment or retribution, although they may appear to be in such categories. Instead they are designed as a means of correction and improvement.

God exercises discipline in respect of His children. Again it needs to be stated that this is distinct from punishment. As the apostle Peter explained, Jesus has clearly and specifically taken upon Himself the wrath of a holy God. This should have come to us on account of our sin (1 Pet. 2:24). Further, the work of God in bringing discipline is not restricted to the Old Testament. The writer to the Hebrews encouraged his readers: 'Endure hardship as discipline; God is treating you as his children' (Heb. 12:7). He added, to show that he knew what he was talking about: 'No discipline seems pleasant at the time, but painful' (Heb. 12:11). As with all genuine discipline, a positive outcome was being sought: 'it produces a harvest of righteousness and peace for those who have been trained by it' (Heb. 12:11).

Giving thought

Back in the time of Haggai the people of God were also being disciplined. But they failed to recognise it. So, having asked a probing question God then speaks through the prophet to point something out: they had failed to face facts. Hence God's repeated instructions: 'Give careful thought to your ways' (Hag. 1:5,7). These facts, as God explained, were that the harvest failures, economic problems and shortages were not just natural events or cycles. God had a part in these situations summed up as follows: 'You expected much, but see, it turned out to be little. What you brought home, I blew away' (Hag. 1:9).

Another question!

On the back of those facts God then launched another probing question! This time it was just one word: 'Why?' By that time the answer was probably obvious, but God spelt it out anyway! 'Because of my house, which remains a ruin, while each of you is busy with your own house' (Hag. 1:9). The troubles and difficulties that the people were suffering (Hag. 1:10–11) were the specific work of God aimed at bringing discipline. This was the means to motivate God's people to change their priorities. They needed, once again, to put Him first in their lives. Temple worship was the principle means by which this was to be shown.

Just like an underperforming sports team, student, employee or motorist, the Jews back in Jerusalem had to face facts. The hardship that they were suffering was God's way of getting them back on track. His people may have failed to grasp the spiritual implications of their neglect, but those 'down to earth' problems could not be escaped. Although it may have seemed harsh, He was actually treating them as His children, having their best interests at heart.

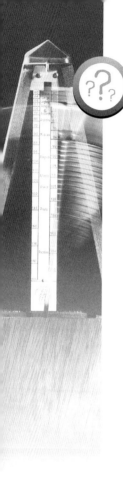

Discussion Starters

1. Hebrews 12:1–6 details God's discipline by describing various forms of motivation. What were these and why was discipline needed?

_____

_____

_____

_____

_____

2. Taking into account your answers to the first question, what do you think were the equivalent sources of motivation to the Jews in Haggai's time?

_____

_____

_____

_____

_____

3. Hebrews 12 also used the backdrop of a race to illustrate what the writer was describing. What aspects would have been a positive motivation to his readers?

_____

_____

_____

_____

_____

4. In what way does encouragement help generate motivation in Hebrews 12:12–13?

_____

_____

_____

_____

_____

5. Why do you think that the discipline described by
Paul in 1 Corinthians 5:11 was so severe?

_____

_____

_____

_____

_____

6. In the case where discipline was carried out (probably
as in 1 Cor. 5, above), what was the aim of it and
what actually happened? See 2 Corinthians 2:5–11.

_____

_____

_____

_____

_____

7. How does Paul's reference to the military, sport and
farming (2 Tim. 2:1–7) link discipline and motivation?

_____

_____

_____

_____

_____

8. What motivation should those in leadership have in
being self-disciplined, and how could that apply to all
Christians, whatever their roles? See Titus 1:5–16; 2:11–15.

_____

_____

_____

_____

_____

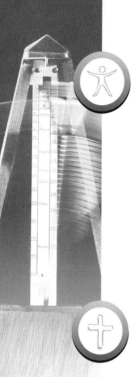

Personal Application

The subject of 'discipline' seems to be less and less popular in our sermons these days, and often only arises in the context of a Christian leader having a major moral lapse or financial irregularity followed by some public redress. The majority of us may feel that this aspect of our relationship with God is not relevant. But, as we have seen, it is something that is actually on God's 'agenda' for all of us. Wisdom is needed both to recognise the form it may take among all the trials of life, and to be ready to respond. Essentially we need to put God first in all things, other priorities falling in behind.

Seeing Jesus in the Scriptures

The words that God gave Haggai to direct His people to face facts were: 'Give careful thought' (Hag. 1:5,7). Jesus used a similar approach when teaching about His kingdom. 'Look at the birds of the air... See how the flowers of the field grow' (Matt. 6:26,28). In each case there was a need to focus on something seen initially as only being incidental. Jesus was pointing out that life was not about trusting in our own resources but in God as our heavenly Father. He then underlined the discipline of seeking first, 'his kingdom and his righteousness' (Matt 6:33). The Jews back in Haggai's time were similarly trusting in their own wealth and pushing God out. Both attitudes needed correcting and involved the element of discipline.

WEEK FOUR

Being Passionate

Icebreaker

Compile a list of the ways in which a group of people who share the same passion can make that passion evident to others around them. How do you think outsiders might be caught up in the issue over which such a group has intense feeling?

Bible Readings

- Haggai 1:12–15
- Proverbs 23:17–18
- John 2:13–17
- 2 Corinthians 5:13–15
- 2 Timothy 1:3–7
- Revelation 3:14–22

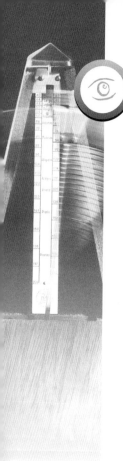

Opening Our Eyes

The tall stranger walked purposefully down the long road. It was through London's East End that he was striding, noticing all that was taking place around him. But he was not only on a physical journey but also a spiritual one. He had found it increasingly difficult to link up with recognised churches because of his concern for the marginalised of society. So he was now on a short-term mission in that part of the city. But that walk saw something more take place. Such was the impression of the squalor and need which he observed that when he returned home to his wife he reportedly stated: 'Darling, I've found my destiny.' Those words marked the passion which stirred the heart of William Booth and initiated the Salvation Army.

Many others have also been moved by situations into which they have been drawn. Much of the social reform, innovation and spiritual renewal seen in Great Britain, and beyond, has arisen from passion arising in men and women. This then motivated them to action.

Stirred by God

Back in 520 BC, following the Jews' return to their homeland, there was a similar response to the serious neglect that was highlighted. This release of passion was not restricted. Although those in leadership seemed to have experienced it first, everyone else soon had the same drive. 'So the LORD stirred up the spirit of Zerubbabel... governor of Judah, and the spirit of Joshua... the high priest, and the spirit of the whole remnant of the people' (Hag. 1:14). That word, 'stirred' brings with it the sense of arousing, awakening and exciting. It was used to explain the reason for Cyrus, king-emperor of Persia, issuing his proclamation allowing the Jews to return from exile in the first place ('moved', Ezra 1:1). Moses also used the word to describe God's intervention in the lives of His people: 'like an eagle that stirs up its nest and hovers over its young' (Deut. 32:11).

For those Jews, previously preoccupied with their own comfort, the result of now being 'stirred' was dramatic. They were motivated to take action. This was serious stuff! 'They came and began to work on the house of the LORD Almighty' (Hag. 1:14). Previous neglect in rebuilding the Temple now gave way to a galvanised response in following God.

Need for action

These were the same people who had been 'moved' to undertake the return journey from exile (same root word as 'stirred' in Ezra 1:5 in several translations). But their renewed passion was not to be seen as something which they had worked up themselves. It had arisen on the back of Haggai's message from God. This had alerted them to the need for action that they initiated just over three weeks later: 'the twenty-fourth day of the sixth month' (Hag. 1:15).

All of this was kick-started by the fact that 'the people feared the LORD' (Hag. 1:12). Hearing that prophetic word from Haggai (including the revelation as to why they had been undergoing hardship) had resulted in a deep awe and reverence of God. A message of encouragement had also been brought: '"I am with you," declares the LORD' (Hag. 1:13). As they consequently obeyed His directive so their passion was awakened. They embarked on God's work, in which they had previously shown no interest. It was a passion that was to enable them to maintain momentum.

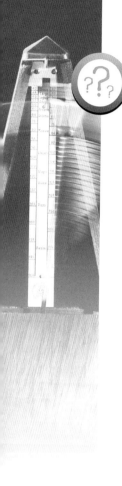

Discussion Starters

1. Why is it necessary for those in leadership (as with Zerubbabel and Joshua) to be passionate about God and His work?

_____

_____

_____

_____

2. Why is it important to step out in obedience to God's direction, as the Jews did when He spoke through Haggai, even though we may not initially have the passion to do so?

_____

_____

_____

_____

3. Do you feel that the encouragement that God is with us (as the Jews were reminded in Haggai 1:13) needs to be linked with passion, and if so, why?

_____

_____

_____

_____

4. Why was the Jews' 'fear' of God a necessary basis for what followed in terms of their subsequent response?

_____

_____

_____

_____

5. What was the importance of all the Jews being passionate about rebuilding the Temple? What problems can occur where only some church members have passion?

_____

_____

_____

_____

_____

6. Haggai records the date on which the rebuilding work actually began (Hag. 1:15). What value was there in doing so? How can this relate to us?

_____

_____

_____

_____

_____

7. What warning could we derive from the message to the Laodicean church (Rev. 3:14–22) for their failure to be passionate?

_____

_____

_____

_____

_____

8. How is the encouragement of Paul to Timothy to 'fan into flame' the gift that was within him (2 Tim. 1:6) also relevant to us?

_____

_____

_____

_____

_____

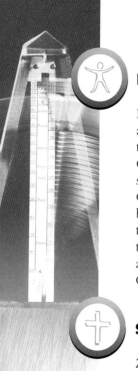

Personal Application

Enthusiasm and passion might not always be viewed as appropriate or positive attributes in church life, but as this passage in Haggai shows, such responses can be God-driven. On the basis of careful attention to what God says, and diligent obedience, they may actually be seen as God-inspired. The writer of Proverbs urges us to 'always be zealous for the fear of the LORD' (Prov. 23:17). To this the apostle Paul adds: 'It is fine to be zealous, provided the purpose is good, and to be so always, not just when I am with you' (Gal. 4:18). Passionately fearing and following God are powerful motivators in our lives as Christians.

Seeing Jesus in the Scriptures

Zerubbabel, the governor of Judah when Haggai brought God's message, was a 'type' of Christ. His passion in obeying God to rebuild the Temple and resume worship prefigured the action of Christ. When the latter drove out the money-changers and traders from Herod's Temple, a particular scripture was recalled: 'zeal for your house consumes me' (Psa. 69:9, also quoted in John 2:17). The governor's action had been motivated by similar zeal for God's glory.

WEEK FIVE

Seeing the Bigger Picture

Icebreaker

Discuss the ways in which drawing comparisons can be a helpful activity to undertake, but could also be discouraging. Particularly look at this in the light of your own experience with, for instance, current service for God compared to last year.

Bible Readings

- Haggai 2:1–9
- Zechariah 4:6–10
- 1 Corinthians 6:18–20
- 2 Corinthians 4:1–17
- Ephesians 2:19–22
- Philippians 1:6

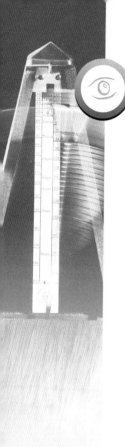

Opening Our Eyes

When work resumed on constructing the new Temple
in Jerusalem, there was one obvious and discouraging
fact. This had been evident 16 years previously when the
foundations had been laid. The account of the celebration
at that time recorded: 'And all the people gave a great
shout of praise to the LORD, because the foundation of
the house of the LORD was laid. But many of the older
priests and Levites and family heads, who had seen the
former temple, wept aloud... while many others shouted
for joy' (Ezra 3:11–12). This new Temple was to bear no
comparison to the size, splendour and workmanship of
Solomon's which had preceded it.

Comparisons

Now, however, those who were old enough to remember
Solomon's Temple (possibly including Haggai himself)
could only draw discouraging comparisons. So why was
God giving these Jews the motivation – both 'carrot' and
'stick' – to build a far-from-impressive structure? God
Himself seemed to want a comparison drawn between
the past and the present. Through Haggai He had asked
specific questions: 'Who of you is left who saw this house
in its former glory? How does it look to you now? Does it
not seem to you like nothing?' (Hag. 2:3).

Those enquiries went unanswered. The response was
obvious. But even as God raised these unpalatable questions
He immediately stepped in with further encouragement.
He told them to, 'Be strong... and work. For I am with you'
(Hag. 2:4). The great name of God, the 'LORD Almighty', was
added to emphasise what He'd just spoken.

Means to an end

Then God directed the people to look back again. They
needed to see the bigger picture. This is because the Jews
had, understandably, been paying attention to the bricks and

mortar in front of them – not a sight to bring motivation! God, however, brought their attention to 'what I covenanted with you when you came out of Egypt' (Hag. 2:5). This was when He declared that He would 'dwell among them' (Exod. 29:46).

For centuries this sense of God dwelling among His people had been portrayed by the tabernacle and then the Temple. The sacrifices offered within them were the route by which God could be approached and sin forgiven. But the Temple was only a means to an end. The moment that Jesus died on the cross, the curtain separating the Holy of Holies from the rest of the Temple would be torn from top to bottom. This signified that there was no further need of temple ritual and sacrifices. Now forgiveness and relationship with God would be specifically through Jesus.

Prophetic

When Haggai then spoke God's word about the time when He would 'shake all nations', he was referring to the spiritual repercussions of Jesus' incarnation: 'and what is desired by all nations will come' (Hag. 2:7). Furthermore, this incarnated Jesus would actually enter this very Temple (subsequently enlarged and beautified under Herod) currently being constructed: 'and I will fill this house with glory.' As a consequence of this: 'The glory of this present house will be greater than the glory of the former house' (Hag. 2:9).

The motivation for Zerubbabel and the Jews was therefore to continue. Although physically less impressive than the previous Temple, it would possess a greater spiritual sense of God's glory. Seeing the bigger picture of what was happening was to provide impetus. They were building in a prophetic sense, anticipating God's promised salvation.

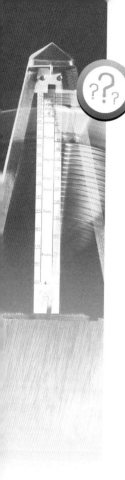

Discussion Starters

1. Zechariah also brought God's word regarding the Temple reconstruction (Zech. 4:6–10). What encouragement did God bring through him when its smaller scale was apparent? How is that relevant to us?

_____

_____

_____

_____

2. God also brought reassurance that this reconstruction would be completed (Zech. 4:9). Why was this important, and how is it applicable to us?

_____

_____

_____

_____

3. Why was it necessary that, at this stage, God said: 'Be strong... For I am with you' (Hag. 2:4)?

_____

_____

_____

_____

4. Why is faith vital in seeing the 'bigger picture' of what God is doing? What was helping build up the Jews' faith during this time?

_____

_____

_____

_____

5. God emphasised the importance of this reconstruction by applying the word 'glory' (Hag. 2:7,9). Why would this help bring a different perspective and how might it also apply to us?

_____

_____

_____

_____

_____

6. What parallels does Paul bring in terms of us being like the physical Temple (Eph. 2:19–22)?

_____

_____

_____

_____

_____

7. Paul described our bodies as being a 'temple' (1 Cor. 6:18–20). What attitude did he want us to have in seeing that perspective?

_____

_____

_____

_____

_____

8. Why was God's closing word through Haggai in this section about 'peace' also important (Hag. 2:9)? How can it relate to us?

_____

_____

_____

_____

_____

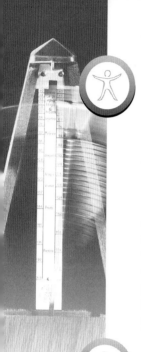

Personal Application

We live in a material world dominated by the information received through our senses. This means that our judgments and conclusions are strongly determined by data that is actually inadequate. There is more going on around us than we realise. And it is God's perspective that counts. We can easily lose heart and become demotivated when failing to see our circumstances as God sees them. We compare situations only with what we think they should be. Just as Haggai was used by God to focus the Jews beyond their immediate impression, so God encourages us to trust Him for the future even though in our eyes this may not look promising.

Seeing Jesus in the Scriptures

These verses provide a glimpse of Jesus, described to these Jews as the 'desired of all nations'. While not as clear a prophecy as others in the Old Testament, it pointed to Him who 'will come'. The effect of His incarnation is described as a distinct one: 'The glory of this present house will be greater than the glory of the former house' (Hag. 2:9). The original Temple, built by Solomon, was visually magnificent and had witnessed God's presence coming down by way of a cloud (2 Chron. 5:13–14). Now God's presence was to be witnessed through His Son Jesus, described by the apostle as one whose 'glory' had been seen (John 1:14).

WEEK SIX

Genuine Commitment

Icebreaker

Draw up a list of the different social media websites of which you are a part or about which you know. Alternatively you could list the community groups in your locality. Discuss what factors would mark out someone as being a 'core member' of such groups.

Bible Readings

- Haggai 2:10–19
- Ecclesiastes 10:1
- Mark 7:1–8
- Mark 12:28–31
- Hebrews 12:1–3
- 1 Peter 1:13–15

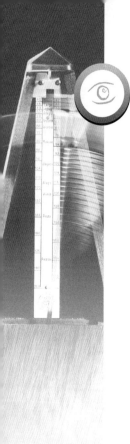

Opening Our Eyes

According to the details on the back of his book, the author knew his subject incredibly well. He had compiled an extremely detailed selection of reflections in respect of... his local professional football team! But this was not a club basking in the glory of ongoing and headline-grabbing success. Quite the opposite. They continually struggled in the lower levels of the national league. But this writer had followed them for many seasons and watched over one thousand matches. This made my own viewing – a dozen over the last few seasons – pale into insignificance! I had attended the same home ground, read their news in the media, and knew their history. But he was a supporter with genuine commitment; I was really only a casual follower.

God's penultimate message to the Jews in Jerusalem through Haggai the prophet drew a similar distinction. 'This people' had engaged in activities that seemed to have 'ticked' all the appropriate boxes. They had responded to the opportunity to return home from exile in Babylon. For the last three months they had been motivated to resume reconstruction of the Temple. All of this had been at a cost. But was this outward action enough? Were they really committed to follow God and His ways?

Further questions

These issues were raised by God by means of yet more probing questions. Directed to the priests, He asked them about the laws of defilement. Would ordinary food become holy when coming into contact with holy meat? The answer was negative. Then He asked if someone who was ceremonially unclean through contact with a dead body then touched any of this ordinary food, would it too be unclean? This time the answer was positive – it would also be defiled according to the law.

Holiness and commitment to God, as brought out through this questioning, was similarly and definitely not transferable. It was also not achieved simply by means of outward actions, even though these Jews had been engaged in reconstruction of the Temple. This was like my own occasional spectating down at the football ground. It did not make me a genuine supporter. There was a distinct 'downside' to this message through Haggai. Contamination was so much more likely to be experienced, whereas holiness and associated commitment to God and His work needed specific effort involving heart-attitude.

Change of heart

So God again directed His people to 'give careful thought' (Hag. 2:15 and again in 2:18). Referring back to His earlier point of poor harvests being His means of discipline and motivation, God indicated a change of heart being needed. Those shortages had arisen in spite of the foundations of the Temple having previously been laid. It had not 'qualified' them as being those who were wholly following God. No deep reformation or commitment had evidently taken place earlier. It's not clear as to whether it now occurred. God's message through Haggai after that interrogation, 'From this day on I will bless you' (Hag. 2:19), may have simply indicated His assured but as yet unmerited blessing to His people.

But God's further probing underlined the need for the Jews to have a deeper relationship with Him and not rely on outward actions. He wanted them to be motivated through their genuine commitment and not simply go through the motions, even though these involved considerable outward effort. Another prophet brought similar words to underline that physical actions were insufficient: 'Rend your heart and not your garments' (Joel 2:13).

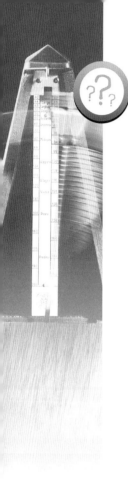

?? **Discussion Starters**

1. What was the problem that Jesus underlined when He addressed the Pharisees in Mark 7:1–8?

_____

_____

_____

_____

_____

2. Why can it seem easier to 'go through the motions', like those Pharisees and the Jews in Haggai's time, than have real commitment to following God?

_____

_____

_____

_____

_____

3. In Mark 12:29–31, why did Jesus stress the need for love and commitment to God to involve the whole of our being and not just part of it?

_____

_____

_____

_____

_____

4. God spoke through Haggai about defilement and consecration. How serious should we be in regard to sin, and how does our attitude towards it reflect our relationship with God? See Hebrews 12:1–3.

_____

_____

_____

_____

5. What does Ecclesiastes say about the effect of sin, however minimal it seems? See Ecclesiastes 10:1 for an example. Why is sin described like this?

_____

_____

_____

_____

_____

6. What area of our lives does Peter point towards in talking about the need to be holy? See 1 Peter 1:13–15.

_____

_____

_____

_____

_____

7. Haggai drew the attention of the Jews to 'Give careful thought' (Hag. 2:15,18). Why should adverse circumstances lead us to self-examination?

_____

_____

_____

_____

_____

8. Why can blessing from God be an important part of us wanting to be genuinely committed to Him?

_____

_____

_____

_____

_____

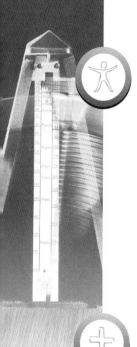

Personal Application

The motivation behind our observable actions is not always clear. We may even fail to fully understand our own motivation partly on account of sin-tainted lives. This is why God spoke through the writer of the Proverbs: 'All a person's ways seem pure to them, but motives are weighed by the LORD' (Prov. 16:2).

For this reason the psalmist prayed that God would 'search' and 'test' him (Psa. 139:23). Let's also allow God to probe us as He did those Jews through Haggai, in order to see below the surface. He wants our commitment to be genuine and be the motivation behind all that we undertake for Him.

Seeing Jesus in the Scriptures

Jesus' ministry included helping people see the need for a deeper and more committed relationship with God. Just as God raised those questions through Haggai, so Jesus' teaching underlined the same point. A barrage of 'woes' was launched on one occasion to the religious leaders of His day. This was regarding the issues of tithing, ceremonial cleaning, and decorating the tombs of the prophets (Matt. 23:23–32). He pointed out that the Pharisees' outward actions were inconsistent with their heart-attitude. As a consequence He labelled them hypocrites. Just as Haggai had also inferred, a change of heart was needed.

WEEK SEVEN

Encouragement

Icebreaker

Personal possessions are sometimes described as having 'intrinsic value'. Think about one or two of your own possessions that may not have much monetary worth but might fall into this category. List the reasons for them being of value to you.

Bible Readings

- Haggai 2:20–23
- 1 Samuel 30:1–6
- Psalm 27
- Acts 27:13–44
- 1 Corinthians 16:13–14
- 2 Thessalonians 2:16–17

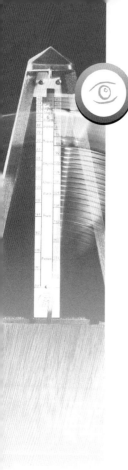

Opening Our Eyes

It can be experienced in very unlikely situations. The hopelessness of a geriatric hospital ward, the email notifying rejection, the failed interview, the devastating phone call. Such 'snap-shots' depicting myriad bleak episodes in life held, for me, a common thread. They were all situations in which encouragement was unexpectedly received.

The interesting thing about 'encouragement' is that it doesn't necessarily change outward circumstances, or at least not immediately. 'High profile' characters in the Bible certainly found this to be the case. Paul, in a storm-tossed boat, received a message from God but still suffered shipwreck. David was threatened by his supporters when terrorists had attacked their camp while they were away on a mission. Yet their families still remained hostage despite David finding comfort in God. But it was the truth about God's love, presence and protection that brought necessary and initial encouragement. This was my experience when finding that a member of staff in that hospital ward was a Christian, and when other believers brought support in those times of severe stress.

Perhaps Zerubbabel, the governor in Jerusalem, would have identified with some of those feelings described above. The urging of God recorded in these two chapters of Haggai was against a backdrop of instability and uncertainty. The geographical area occupied by these returning Jews had been small, comprising a tiny patch of the Persian Empire. In addition, their rebuilding projects had not gone unnoticed. Significant opposition from neighbouring warlords had arisen – these confrontations were detailed in the books of Ezra and Nehemiah. The former actually referred to the motivational prophecies of both Haggai and Zechariah (Ezra 5:1–2).

God's message

The final prophecy of God through Haggai was brought on the same day as those earlier questions (see Week Six). But this time it was God speaking specifically to Zerubbabel. This was a message of encouragement that started by declaring the power of God to overcome the enemies of His people. It must have been particularly reassuring in the context of the Jews' impotence, caught up in the power-struggles of succeeding empires, and in that grim environment.

But God also spoke to Zerubbabel on a personal level, addressing him as His 'servant' and describing him as His 'signet ring'. The latter spoke powerfully of both security and authority. This was because such a ring – into which a stone was set, engraved with the owner's symbol – was used to authenticate documents, including royal commands. In that unstable and uncertain era it was God's way of underlining the fact that He would neither forget nor abandon His people.

Valued

This message to Zerubbabel was a guarantee of God's power behind His direction in respect of the Temple being rebuilt. The declaration of this being made by the 'Lord Almighty' added emphasis. Encouragement from realising the value that God placed on Zerubbabel and His people would have been a powerful motivator.

Although Haggai's brief prophecy – it came over a period of about four months – ended somewhat abruptly, it did so on this very 'upbeat' note. God was speaking over His people to encourage and motivate. He wanted them to maintain momentum in building His Temple. This was a prophetic demonstration of His work on this earth and illustrative of people wanting to follow Him. God hasn't changed. He still wants people like you and me to maintain momentum, have ongoing commitment to Him and to be involved in serving Him in whatever form it may take.

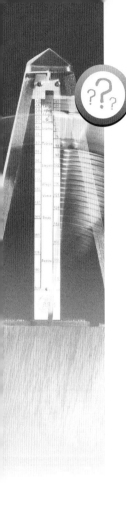

Discussion Starters

1. Why can encouragement be a powerful motivation when undertaking difficult tasks?

_____

_____

_____

_____

2. Why is encouragement directly from God particularly motivating for us? What have your own experiences been?

_____

_____

_____

_____

3. God spoke to those Jews in very positive ways: 'I am with you', 'Be strong', 'Do not fear', 'I will bless you' (Hag. 1:13; 2:4–5,19). How would these have brought encouragement and motivation?

_____

_____

_____

_____

4. Why was it important for Zerubbabel to hear that he was God's 'signet ring' and that he was 'chosen'? What would have been the likely impact on him?

_____

_____

_____

_____

5. Why is it important that we understand our value to God? See Malachi 3:17; Isaiah 49:16; 1 Peter 2:9.

_____

_____

_____

_____

6. What motivation can be derived from knowing that we are special to God?

_____

_____

_____

_____

7. Read 2 Thessalonians 2:16–17. Why might Paul have been praying for encouragement for this particular group of Christians?

_____

_____

_____

_____

8. By what means might God now bring us motivation through encouragement?

_____

_____

_____

_____

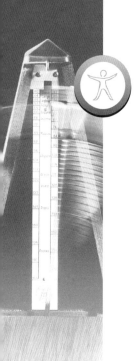

Personal Application

Haggai's prophecy highlighted different ways by which God motivated His people. Over that short time He had asked probing questions (several of them!) and pointed out some awkward facts. God challenged them in respect of passion and commitment, and also steered them to focus beyond their horizon. But interspersed with these were His words of reassurance and affirmation. This culminated in specifically addressing Zerubbabel.

God still brings encouragement to us. This can arise through His Word, other Christians, or through specific circumstances that bless us. Let's be alert to these and other forms of encouragement. Like Zerubbabel, we may also need to 'hang in there'. The psalmist put it this way: 'Wait for the LORD; be strong and take heart and wait for the LORD' (Psa. 27:14).

Seeing Jesus in the Scriptures

Zerubbabel was described by God as one who was His 'servant' and whom He had 'chosen' (Hag. 2:23). This reflected the position of Jesus, of whom God the Father stated: 'Here is my servant, whom I uphold, my chosen one in whom I delight; I will put my Spirit on him' (Isa. 42:1). The apostle Peter also wrote of Jesus: 'He was chosen before the creation of the world' (1 Pet. 1:20).

Zerubbabel's name was subsequently listed among those who were the human ancestors of Jesus (Matt. 1:12–13; Luke 3:27). Like Jesus, he was working out God's purposes in a dark spiritual environment, needing affirmation from God as Jesus Himself received when He was baptised (Luke 3:22).

Leader's Notes

Icebreaker

Many reasons can lie behind appointments being noted in our diaries. A summons to attend for jury service at a specified date is not easily put off, whereas some social arrangements are open to negotiation. But it's the motivation behind them that's being considered. Some have financial penalties for failure to carry through. Others have motivation arising from self-interest (such as a hospital consultant's appointment) or pleasurable experience (meeting a good friend).

Aim of the Session

To recognise that God's timing of events forms an element of motivation in undertaking tasks for Him.

Discussion Starters

1. The pressured and fast-paced lifestyles with which many people have to contend can cause our minds to be full of data and memories that are not easily accessed. Recording our experiences of God, together with details of timing, can be a positive means of encouragement and motivation for the future, as past events are reviewed.

2. The psalmist states: 'As for God, His way is perfect: the LORD's word is flawless' (Psa. 18:30). His perfect knowledge of all that takes place – past, present and future – means that He knows the best time

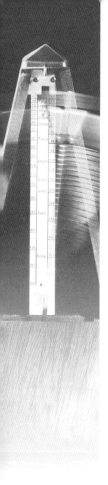

to act. His patience means that He doesn't act too early; His mercy means that He never holds back (2 Pet. 3:9; Isa. 30:19).

3.   While no reasons are specified in this prophecy, other scriptures describe God's nature, which determines His action. He is described as 'patient', 'long-suffering', 'gracious', 'slow to anger', and acting 'quickly'. He knows our human frailty and is 'merciful'. These attributes would have come into play, together with the fact that He will get the glory for all that He's done (including the timing, see Rev. 4:11).

4.   Psalm 139 is a reminder that we can know God's presence in every situation. This is important when living in a material world in which our lives seem inevitably shaped and influenced by other people – both those known to us and those who are remote. But in that context it also points to God's overruling control in our lives from the day of our birth to that of our death. Psalm 31 states that all of our times are in His hands (v15). This can provide a general motivation to trust God in all circumstances.

5.   Believing that God has been ultimately responsible for our birth, and the time that it occurred, brings reassurance that He has plans and purposes for us. That concept was brought to Jeremiah and motivated him even though he was reticent (see Jer. 1:5).

6.   The speed at which life passes and the pace at which it's lived can make us oblivious to what we are accomplishing. Psalm 90 reminds us of life's transitory nature and brings a motivation to focus on the things that are really important.

7. When we recognise the value of time – it can't be saved up, spent later, sold off or slowed down – then each day needs to be spent purposefully and carefully. It also needs to be spent in the light of eternity, even after a long life span (see Psa. 90). What happens after death is determined by time spent here, and our response to God's 'agenda' for our lives.

8. Perhaps the 'rubber hits the road' in respect of motivation when considering the need to spend regular time in prayer and Bible reading. Many pressures and obstacles arise that curtail motivation in this area of Christian life. But making a predetermined daily or weekly 'slot' in our agenda can be a powerful motivator in achieving this goal of interacting with God.

Week Two: Probing Questions

Icebreaker

Although most questions are asked with a view to obtaining information, others are raised with different objectives. A teacher is likely to ask a student for information to ascertain if certain knowledge is held; a doctor to determine a diagnosis. Questions can be vital in assessing a situation, or trivial and completely incidental. Some may not even require an answer or a precise reply, seeking only general opinions or possibilities.

Aim of the Session

To understand that 'probing' questions by God can generate motivation.

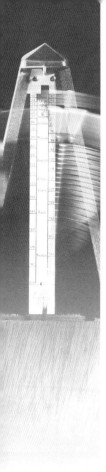

Discussion Starters

1. The question raised by God through Haggai is recorded simply by means of words. There is no indication as to the prophet's tone of voice, appearance or the surroundings in which it was delivered. But there are suggestions that it was delivered forcibly. It was introduced by the use of God's name, 'the LORD Almighty', underlining His total sovereign reign and rule. The fact that He had heard and seen everything was a further factor. There seemed no doubt that Haggai had approached the civil and religious leaders with a fearless confidence that it was God's message that he was delivering. Also relevant would have been the fact that God alone had been responsible for the Jews' wonderful restoration from exile only 16 years previously.

2. The statement that prefaced God's question was quoting what people were saying. This showed that other things had a higher priority in their lives. They had not even bothered to set a date in their own 'diary' as to when rebuilding work should recommence. This pointed to a complete failure to recognise the importance of this task. Their greater concern was their own comfort and not the worship of God.

3. Questions are a particularly good way of placing the onus on the person or people being interrogated. Articulating a reply, perhaps giving information or reasoning behind a course of action, can reveal inadequacies or wrong perceptions, which can then be addressed.

4. Isaiah was directing God's people to think more deeply. They were pointed to consider the impotence of the 'gods' of other nations around them (Isa. 40:18–20). Further, they were questioned to recognise the clear power of God over nations and creation (Isa. 40:12–17,21–26).

5. By quoting back their own comment, God was showing His people that He wasn't distant, uncaring or ignorant of what they were experiencing. Subsequent verses showed both His power and His concern so that His people could draw strength from being close to Him.

6. God was not questioning Adam in order to establish his physical location but his spiritual condition. The latter was now one of distancing and hiding himself from God. So God was motivating Adam to take stock of his relationship with Him and how this had changed, as revealed by answers to subsequent questions.

7. This paralysed man was not alone, but lying alongside others in an environment of sickness and disease. He may have therefore become adjusted or accustomed to his condition, particularly on account of its longevity. Any healing that he may have received, either from the waters being stirred or by Jesus, would have radically altered his lifestyle. So Jesus' question was causing him to think about his motivation behind seeking a miraculous intervention.

8. Jesus was actually walking out of Jericho and away from Bartimaeus when the latter cried out to Him for mercy. There was a large crowd together with the disciples surrounding Jesus. Despite the initial rebuke of people around him, Bartimaeus persisted. So Jesus' question could actually have motivated him to have anticipation and hope of being healed.

Week Three: Facing Facts

Icebreaker

The terms now used, such as mentoring, tuition, training and coaching, suggest different ways to enhance performance. They can indicate both the resources being used (such as one-to-one involvement in mentoring and life-coaching) and the style that's being adopted (such as step-by-step guidance through instruction and coaching). Each has an element of motivation and discipline.

Aim of the Session

To show that discipline is an integral part of Christian life and a means of motivation.

Discussion Starters

1. Hebrews was a letter written to struggling Christians. Motivation was needed on account of weariness and discouragement in this spiritual 'race'. They were encouraged to note those who had lived before them and whose persevering faith had seen obstacles overcome (see Heb. 11). They were urged to 'fix' their focus on Jesus, who endured the cross. Discipline had come because they had not fully resisted sin and they had failed to remember that God could work through hardship for their benefit.

2. The returning Jews could have derived encouragement and motivation from the circumstances in which that restoration had taken place. Their more distant history, reminders of which were presented through their feasts, was designed to produce the same effect. Focusing on their leaders like Moses and Joshua ('shadows' of Christ, Heb. 8:5) would also have been motivating.

3. There is motivation in that the 'race' is 'marked out', the life of faith being set out in the examples of the previous chapter (Heb. 11). Those people were clear 'witnesses' of God's work in the lives of those who trusted Him. Jesus was also going ahead of them at the end of the 'race'. Motivation also arose in knowing that God enables His people to continue by strengthening and restoring them (Heb. 12–13).

4. The writer of Hebrews was aware that his readers were not in a 'good place'. They had 'feeble arms' and 'weak knees'. But encouragement to put things right ('make level paths for your feet') indicated a belief that they could do so. This would have been a powerful motivation to them, and us, to acknowledge weaknesses and experience God's help.

5. The failing of this Christian to whom Paul was directing that discipline should be exercised was both public and condoned by the Corinthian church. So severe action was needed as a means of motivating the man himself to repent, and to show everyone that his behaviour was unacceptable.

6. It seems that most of the Corinthian Christians had totally disassociated themselves from this man whose sin had been so public. It had achieved the aim of motivating him to 'sorrow'. But the action against him had been overdone. Consequently there was the possibility of him being 'overwhelmed by... sorrow'. Paul now wanted forgiveness, comfort and affirming love to be shown.

7. Motivation is indicated by Paul wanting to please God, paralleled by a soldier pleasing his 'commanding officer'. For that reason there is no involvement in 'civilian affairs' (2 Tim. 2:4). There is

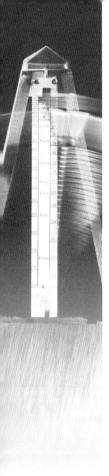

also focus on competing as an 'athlete... according to the rules' (2 Tim. 2:5). A reward, as with a farmer receiving a share of the crops, also brings motivation (2 Tim 2:6).

8. Self-motivation, linked to 'self-control' (Titus 1:5–16), is needed because an elder 'manages God's household' (v7). An example is also presented since self-control is to be taught to older and younger men (Titus 2:2,6,12)! Motivation to live 'upright and godly lives' is seen as applicable to all believers, arising from the teaching and authority of these elders (Titus 1:8; 2:12,15).

Week Four: Being Passionate

Icebreaker

Passion and enthusiasm are, by their nature, displayed in obvious ways. They tend to dominate conversation, and take up time, energy and resources. The motivation that arises through such outworking can be very infectious.

Aim of the Session

To see the importance and proper place of enthusiasm in bringing motivation to the Christian life.

Discussion Starters

1. The importance of leaders in showing passion is mainly because they act as examples to those being led. The apostle Paul frequently referred to his own example and that of those whom he appointed as elders: 'set an example for the believers in speech, in conduct, in love, in faith and in purity' (1 Tim. 4:12). He also described his driving passion for Christ.

2. God's call on our lives is not dependent upon our feelings. Paul directed that Timothy should be prepared (for God's work) 'in season and out of season', whatever things looked like outwardly or within (2 Tim. 4:2). On one occasion Paul wrote that he 'despaired of life itself' (2 Cor. 1:8). Yet underlying his actions was the fact that 'Christ's love compels us' (2 Cor. 5:14).

3. These were the first words of encouragement through Haggai to the Jews: 'I am with you.' The words seemed to come as a separate message at a later point. But they were from the Lord Almighty, the Lord of hosts. In an environment of being alone, vulnerable and with few resources, the fact that God made this declaration would have enthused and motivated His people.

4. The 'fear' of God arose from a reminder of all His mighty acts in the past. These included the Exodus, the conquest of the Promised Land, deliverances through the Judges, and the more recent exile and restoration. All of these actions showed His power and the dependability of His promises. Reverence and awe arising from His commandments to be holy and obedient would have motivated the Jews to return to His ways.

5. The failure of everyone to be passionate and motivated results in energy and momentum being drained away. Twelve representatives of the tribes of Israel were sent to spy out the Promised Land. But only two came back with an enthusiastic report of confidence in God's power to deliver the land to His people. This division proved catastrophic. The demotivating report of the majority was believed and 40 years of wandering in the wilderness ensued (Num. 13:26–14:1).

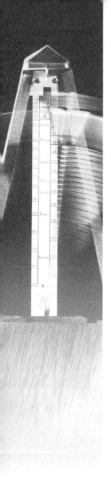

6. Recording the date on which the reconstruction work recommenced would have set a marker. It enabled progress to be monitored and generated enthusiasm. What would have been accomplished over that period could have been easily overlooked. This aspect was to be subsequently hinted at by Haggai. When bringing a further prophetic word he described the Temple foundations being specifically laid at the time of Ezra (Hag. 2:15,18).

7. The Christians in Laodicea were described as being 'lukewarm – neither hot nor cold' (Rev. 3:16). As a consequence of their lack of enthusiasm, or even of deliberate backsliding, Jesus was about to 'spit' them out of His mouth. They were called to 'be earnest and repent' (Rev. 3:19) and to show passion in opening the door to Jesus (instead of being self-sufficient) to 'eat' with Him (Rev. 3:20).

8. Paul encouraged Timothy because the latter was affected by fear, timidity and consciousness of his youth. He was being urged to stir up his God-given gifting for the benefit of the church. God wants us to be passionate about His work and the specific gifts that He has given each of us to carry this out.

Week Five: Seeing the Bigger Picture

Icebreaker

Considerable motivation can be generated when we realise what progress we may have achieved over a period of time. However, if no movement is apparent then it can cause a loss of heart.

Aim of the Session

To realise the importance of seeing situations from God's perspective and the motivation that such a viewpoint can generate.

Discussion Starters

1. Two particular declarations from God stand out: "'Not by might nor by power, but by my Spirit," says the LORD Almighty', and 'Who dares despise the day of small things, since the seven eyes of the LORD that range throughout the earth will rejoice when they see the chosen capstone in the hand of Zerubbabel?' (Zech. 4:6,10). The first is relevant and motivating because it's a reminder that work for God is not dependent upon our own ability. The second underlines our need to avoid judging 'success' or 'progress' on the basis of what we see in physical terms.

2. The Jews of Haggai and Zechariah's time needed to know that their work was worthwhile. Seeing the bigger picture, however indistinct, would motivate them – particularly in knowing that God would help them finish the task. Paul brings similar encouragement to us (Phil. 1:6).

3. This reminder of God's presence was encouraging and motivating to the Jews. They were being urged to put effort and resources into a rebuilding project that did not look worthwhile to them. But this specific declaration helped them see that God considered it important and that there was to be a particular value in it, albeit in the distant future.

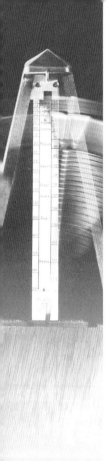

4. Our natural senses are unable to discern God's 'bigger picture'. It is only by trusting in Him that we can have such a viewpoint, although – as with these Jews – the precise details may not be clear. But God's word, as also experienced by these Jews in Jerusalem through Haggai, brings reassurance and motivation to follow His direction even though it may not make sense to us.

5. The Jews would have viewed this rebuilding work in very practical terms. But God, using the word 'glory', showed that there was a wonderful spiritual dimension to what was taking place. Paul described us as being 'jars of clay' in whom God's 'treasure' was placed (2 Cor. 4:7). We may not value ourselves or our efforts but God reveals His power through our inadequacies.

6. The picture is of us being like a temple with foundations (the apostles and prophets) and Christ as the 'chief cornerstone'. We are indwelt by God's Holy Spirit in the same way that God had promised Haggai that His presence would fill the Temple.

7. This description was initially used when writing to Christians in Corinth, where promiscuity was rife. In viewing our bodies as the 'temple of the Holy Spirit' our behaviour will be governed by a different perspective.

8. In the turmoil of emotions, uncertainties and considerable practical demands, this word from God ('peace', from the Hebrew 'shalom') denoted wholeness and completeness. The Jews would have derived both comfort and confidence from this message. The same is true for us when our work for God may seem disjointed and incomplete.

Week Six: Genuine Commitment

Icebreaker

Many people respond to 'invitations' or are drawn into signing up with social media sites or community groups. However, active involvement is something else! It can involve regular scrutiny of ongoing postings, responding to specific messages, and ongoing contribution to discussion threads. Having a name, picture and personal details posted up, but no further interaction, is not sufficient to be 'engaged' in this form of media.

Aim of the Session

This session links motivation to the need for a deep commitment to God, not a superficial relationship based simply on actions.

Discussion Starters

1.   Jesus pinpointed the inconsistency in what the religious leaders said and did, with the attitude of their hearts. It was the latter which counted. The Pharisees wrongly considered that outward and meticulous observance of the Law was the means by which to have a deep relationship with God. The Jews at the time of Haggai, having a similar approach, also needed to see that heart-attitude was more important.

2.   Outward actions can easily become a 'box-ticking' exercise, formal and dispassionate. They can also become an automatic and unthinking operation. This kind of lukewarm approach was condemned by Jesus when He addressed the Christians of the church in Laodicea (Rev. 3:15–18).

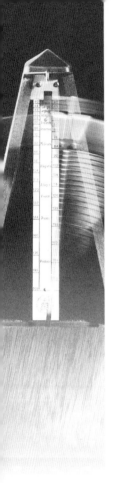

3. God commends people of integrity. This is a quality linked to our lifestyle (Prov. 10:9; 11:3; 13:6). It represents a person's mind, body, soul and spirit working in unity, not being 'out of sync'. So our commitment to God is to involve every part of us, with the result that we become like Jesus, who was specifically described as being a man of integrity (Mark 12:14).

4. Sin needs to be treated very seriously and sorted out. Only when we 'throw off everything that hinders' and deal with sin can we 'run the race marked out for us' (Heb. 12:1). This is linked with the need to be 'fixing our eyes on Jesus' (Heb. 12:2). Disentangling ourselves from sin reflects our desire to follow Jesus. The Jews at the time of Haggai had been distracted by self-interest and seemingly had only an intermittent relationship with God. Discipline had been brought by God to motivate them to have a genuine commitment.

5. However minimal sin may appear, its effects are devastating. The letters in the New Testament included consistent urging for their readers to deal with sin in its many forms.

6. The apostle Peter highlighted the need for our thought-life to be 'holy'. While outward actions might be kept in check, the thoughts that we allow our hearts and minds to dwell upon can be toxic. Jesus, again, drew attention to this disparity between observable behaviour and unseen desires (Matt. 15:19).

7. Circumstances, as pointed out through Haggai, could be God's means of drawing attention to attitudes and behaviour needing corrective action.

8. Our desire should be for a deeper relationship with God, distinct from just wanting His blessing. However, in whatever form He may deem appropriate, blessings are the outworking of His Father-heart and a powerful driver to seek Him. The psalmist linked a deep and appreciative relationship with God and His many blessings in Psalm 103 (especially vv1–6).

Week Seven: Encouragement

Icebreaker

Some possessions are treasured not because of their financial value, but because of positive memories they evoke or because they are gifts from people who have been special to us. They might also be reminders of experiencing God in a special way. These can be sources of encouragement and give us a 'lift'.

Aim of the Session

Encouragement is vital in our lives as Christians and in motivating us to walk with God. This final session looks at how God brings such encouragement.

Discussion Starters

1. Loss of heart in undertaking difficult tasks or facing daunting obstacles can sap our physical energy and emotional drive. Encouragement – the bringing of courage to our hearts – can enable us to press on and overcome barriers. Paul wrote, 'be courageous' (1 Cor. 16:13) and the writer to the Hebrews wrote, 'So do not throw away your confidence' (Heb. 10:35). He also wrote of the need to regularly 'encourage one another' (Heb. 3:13; 10:25).

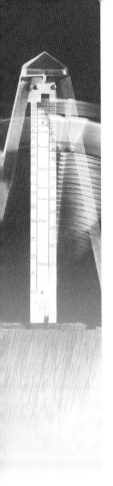

2. Ultimate encouragement comes from God. This is because He has power over every situation, knowing the end from the beginning. When David was in that dire situation it is recorded: 'But David found strength in the LORD his God' (1 Sam. 30:6, the King James Version says he 'encouraged himself'). Similarly, Paul passed on encouragement in that storm-tossed ship: 'But now I urge you to keep up your courage... Last night an angel of the God to whom I belong... stood beside me and said, "Do not be afraid, Paul..." So keep up your courage, men, for I have faith in God that it will happen just as he told me' (Acts 27:22–25).

3. God's words for Zerubbabel would have brought assurance and affirmation both to him and to those whom he led. They were living in a hostile environment and had been victims of aggression for centuries. Their return home and rebuilding of the Temple had been undertaken without significant external support. Being aware of God's presence and protection would have been vital in motivating them to continue this work.

4. Unlike the previous leaders of Israel, such as Moses, Joshua and David, Zerubbabel had not experienced ongoing demonstrations of God's intervention. So God's word would have brought considerable reassurance and empowerment. God's further word through Zechariah, '"Not by might nor by power, but by my Spirit," says the LORD Almighty' (Zech. 4:6), would have counteracted feelings of inadequacy and weakness.

5. We live in a world and spiritual environment that places great value on status, achievement, possessions, charismatic personality and being a 'celebrity'. The number of Facebook friends and Twitter followers is the means by which many people gauge their worth. But God's values are different! What He says of us is what really counts!

6. Growing in appreciation of God's love, care and value builds our sense of real worth and identity. This motivates our trusting obedience upon God, helping us undertake His calling. This is even though we may not amount to much as far as the world is concerned.

7. Paul saw the need for encouragement so that Christians living in a hostile society could achieve God's purposes in their lives 'in every good deed and word' (2 Thess. 2:17). This added to earlier encouragement: 'The one who calls you is faithful, and he will do it' (1 Thess. 5:24).

8. Reading the Bible is the prime source of encouragement. God also speaks through many and various other means but particularly through other Christians, the quietness of our own hearts, and as we worship Him.

Be inspired by God.
Every day.

Cover to Cover Every Day

In-depth study of the Bible, book by book. Part of a five-year series. Available as an email subscription or on eBook and Kindle.

One-year subscriptions available for all titles

Every Day with Jesus

The popular daily Bible reading notes by Selwyn Hughes.

Inspiring Women Every Day

Daily insight and encouragement written by women for women.

Life Every Day

Lively Bible notes, with Jeff Lucas' wit and wisdom.

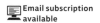

Latest Resource

Jacob – Taking Hold of God's Blessing
by Sarah Evans

This seven-week study guide takes you through the life of Jacob. You'll consider Jacob's experiences as a son, brother, husband and father, and how he wrestled with the God he loved to take hold of His blessing. Be encouraged to take hold of the blessing God has for you.

72-page booklet, 210x148mm
ISBN: 978-1-78259-685-1

The Popular *Cover to Cover* Bible Study Series

1 Corinthians
Growing a Spirit-filled church
ISBN: 978-1-85345-374-8

2 Corinthians
Restoring harmony
ISBN: 978-1-85345-551-3

1 Peter
Good reasons for hope
ISBN: 978-1-78259-088-0

2 Peter
Living in the light of God's promises
ISBN: 978-1-78259-403-1

1 Timothy
Healthy churches –
effective Christians
ISBN: 978-1-85345-291-8

23rd Psalm
The Lord is my shepherd
ISBN: 978-1-85345-449-3

2 Timothy and Titus
Vital Christianity
ISBN: 978-1-85345-338-0

Abraham
Adventures of faith
ISBN: 978-1-78259-089-7

Acts 1–12
Church on the move
ISBN: 978-1-85345-574-2

Acts 13–28
To the ends of the earth
ISBN: 978-1-85345-592-6

Barnabas
Son of encouragement
ISBN: 978-1-85345-911-5

Bible Genres
Hearing what the Bible really says
ISBN: 978-1-85345-987-0

Daniel
Living boldly for God
ISBN: 978-1-85345-986-3

David
A man after God's own heart
ISBN: 978-1-78259-444-4

Ecclesiastes
Hard questions and
spiritual answers
ISBN: 978-1-85345-371-7

Elijah
A man and his God
ISBN: 978-1-85345-575-9

Elisha
A lesson in faithfulness
ISBN: 978-1-78259-494-9

Ephesians
Claiming your inheritance
ISBN: 978-1-85345-229-1

Esther
For such a time as this
ISBN: 978-1-85345-511-7

Fruit of the Spirit
Growing more like Jesus
ISBN: 978-1-85345-375-5

Galatians
Freedom in Christ
ISBN: 978-1-85345-648-0

God's Rescue Plan
Finding God's fingerprints
on human history
ISBN: 978-1-85345-294-9

Great Prayers of the Bible
Applying them to our lives today
ISBN: 978-1-85345-253-6

Haggai
Motivating God's people
ISBN: 978-1-78259-686-8

Hebrews
Jesus – simply the best
ISBN: 978-1-85345-337-3

Hosea
The love that never fails
ISBN: 978-1-85345-290-1

Isaiah 1–39
Prophet to the nations
ISBN: 978-1-85345-510-0

Isaiah 40-66
Prophet of restoration
ISBN: 978-1-85345-550-6

Jacob
Taking hold of God's blessing
ISBN: 978-1-78259-685-1

James
Faith in action
ISBN: 978-1-85345-293-2

Jeremiah
The passionate prophet
ISBN: 978-1-85345-372-4

John's Gospel
Exploring the seven miraculous
signs
ISBN: 978-1-85345-295-6

Joseph
The power of forgiveness and
reconciliation
ISBN: 978-1-85345-252-9

Joshua 1-10
Hand in hand with God
ISBN: 978-1-85345-542-7

Judges 1-8
The spiral of faith
ISBN: 978-1-85345-681-7

Judges 9-21
Learning to live God's way
ISBN: 978-1-85345-910-8

Luke
A prescription for living
ISBN: 978-1-78259-270-9

Mark
Life as it is meant to be lived
ISBN: 978-1-85345-233-8

Mary
The mother of Jesus
ISBN: 978-1-78259-402-4

Moses
Face to face with God
ISBN: 978-1-85345-336-6

Names of God
Exploring the depths of
God's character
ISBN: 978-1-85345-680-0

Nehemiah
Principles for life
ISBN: 978-1-85345-335-9

Parables
Communicating God on earth
ISBN: 978-1-85345-340-3

Philemon
From slavery to freedom
ISBN: 978-1-85345-453-0

Philippians
Living for the sake of the gospel
ISBN: 978-1-85345-421-9

Prayers of Jesus
Hearing His heartbeat
ISBN: 978-1-85345-647-3

Proverbs
Living a life of wisdom
ISBN: 978-1-85345-373-1

Revelation 1-3
Christ's call to the Church
ISBN: 978-1-85345-461-5

Revelation 4-22
The Lamb wins! Christ's final
victory
ISBN: 978-1-85345-411-0

Rivers of Justice
Responding to God's call to
righteousness today
ISBN: 978-1-85345-339-7

Ruth
Loving kindness in action
ISBN: 978-1-85345-231-4

The Armour of God
Living in His strength
ISBN: 978-1-78259-583-0

The Beatitudes
Immersed in the grace
of Christ
ISBN: 978-1-78259-495-6

The Covenants
God's promises and their
relevance today
ISBN: 978-1-85345-255-0

The Creed
Belief in action
SBN: 978-1-78259-202-0

The Divine Blueprint
God's extraordinary power
in ordinary lives
ISBN: 978-1-85345-292-5

The Holy Spirit
Understanding and experiencing
Him
ISBN: 978-1-85345-254-3

The Image of God
His attributes and character
ISBN: 978-1-85345-228-4

The Kingdom
Studies from Matthew's Gospel
ISBN: 978-1-85345-251-2

The Letter to the Colossians
In Christ alone
ISBN: 978-1-855345-405-9

The Letter to the Romans
Good news for everyone
ISBN: 978-1-85345-250-5

The Lord's Prayer
Praying Jesus' way
ISBN: 978-1-85345-460-8

The Prodigal Son
Amazing grace
ISBN: 978-1-85345-412-7

The Second Coming
Living in the light of Jesus' return
ISBN: 978-1-85345-422-6

The Sermon on the Mount
Life within the new covenant
ISBN: 978-1-85345-370-0

Thessalonians
Building Church in changing
times
ISBN: 978-1-78259-443-7

The Ten Commandments
Living God's Way
ISBN: 978-1-85345-593-3

The Uniqueness of our Faith
What makes Christianity
distinctive?
ISBN: 978-1-85345-232-1

For current prices or to order, visit **www.cwr.org.uk/store**
Available online or from Christian bookshops.

SmallGroup central

All of our small group ideas and resources in one place

Online:

www.smallgroupcentral.org.uk
is filled with free video teaching,
tools, articles and a whole host
of ideas.

On the road:

A range of seminars themed for
small groups can be brought to
your local community. Contact us at
hello@smallgroupcentral.org.uk

In print:

Books, study guides and DVDs
covering an extensive list of themes,
Bible books and life issues.

Log on and find out more at:
www.smallgroupcentral.org.uk

Courses and events

Waverley Abbey College

Publishing and media

Conference facilities

Transforming lives

CWR's vision is to enable people to experience personal transformation through applying God's Word to their lives and relationships.

Our Bible-based training and resources help people around the world to:
• Grow in their walk with God
• Understand and apply Scripture to their lives
• Resource themselves and their church
• Develop pastoral care and counselling skills
• Train for leadership
• Strengthen relationships, marriage and family life and much more.

Our insightful writers provide daily Bible reading notes and other resources for all ages, and our experienced course designers and presenters have gained an international reputation for excellence and effectiveness.

CWR's Training and Conference Centres in Surrey and East Sussex, England, provide excellent facilities in idyllic settings – ideal for both learning and spiritual refreshment.

CWR Applying God's Word
to everyday life and relationships

CWR, Waverley Abbey House,
Waverley Lane, Farnham,
Surrey GU9 8EP, UK

Telephone: **+44 (0)1252 784700**
Email: **info@cwr.org.uk**
Website: **www.cwr.org.uk**

Registered Charity No. 294387
Company Registration No. 1990308